Fight Like Hell

A COLLECTION OF POEMS

Miabel J. Self

Copyright © 2017 by Miabel J. Self.

All rights reserved. No part of this publication may be reproduced, distributed or transmitted in any form or by any means, including photocopying, recording, or other electronic or mechanical methods, without the prior written permission of the publisher, except in the case of brief quotations embodied in critical reviews and certain other noncommercial uses permitted by copyright law.

Miabel J. Self
www.poetsperspective.com

Front Cover Illustration © Jeanette Spencer
Book Cover Design © Hannah Rose Creative

Book Layout ©2017 ReneeFisher.com.

Fight Like Hell / Miabel J. Self. —1st ed.
ISBN 978-1544070346

Contents

Will it Start With You?	1
Stand Tall Little One, You Do Make a Difference	5
You're Not Mine	7
Possibilities	11
Transitioning	15
The Lesson	19
Perspective on Perception	25
An Everlasting Remembrance	29
The One	31
The Perfect Love Story	35
Wondering About Wondering	39
What You Left Behind	41
Live Through It	45
About The Author	48

Dedication

To all of the girls.
All over the world, who are fighting their fight.
You are never alone.
You are never deserted.
You are strong.
You are capable.
You are enough.
And you can be the change.
Live every minute, love with all you have, and always fight like hell.

Acknowledgements

To my mother. Thank you mom for cheering me on when I am low, for pushing me to my fullest potential in everything I do, and for being an amazing mother and best friend. You help shape every aspect of my being. You have made me into the strong and confident person I am today. I could not be where I am today without your support and love.

To my dad and my sister, Haley. Thank you for reminding me to laugh when I sometimes forget how it's even possible.

To my amazing grandparents, Mimi and Pawpaw. Thank you so much for all that you have done for me. Your continuous and boundless love for me, inspires me, and shows me how I wish to love others. I am so blessed to have you as my grandparents.

To the three best English teachers I have ever had the pleasure of learning from. Thank you Ms. O'Bryant for pushing me to excel in my writing capabilities, and for teaching me that there is no such thing as getting a 100 on an essay because writing is something that can never be finished to perfection, and for showing me that its okay to be flawed. Also, thank you Mrs. Cox for showing me how to embrace my weirdness and that I can be nice, pretty, and smart at the same time. Additionally, thank you Ms. Muzney for first introducing me to poetry and teaching me how writing can be used as an outlet. Thank you for teaching me to love and appreciate my own thoughts and words. I would not be here without each of you.

To Dr. Tardy and family. Thank you Dr. Tardy for being the best doctor I have ever known. With this disease we both know I have known a lot of them. Thank you for helping me keep my faith and always showing me that I am more than just my disease. Also, thank you to Dr. Tardy's family because of all those long days that he spends with me, caring for me, I just wanted to tell you that without him, I would not be here today.

To Mr. Davidson. My mentor and MacTEACH Sponsor. Thank you for showing me that my words do make a difference and for instilling confidence in me, my abilities, and my future. By example, you have shown me the importance of education through peer-to-peer tutoring with the at-risk children in my community. The bonds made through this program will last a lifetime. You have made me a much stronger human being in more ways than just one. Thank you for pushing me to my greatest potential and for making a difference in my life.

To Mrs. Jackson, my middle school AVID teacher, thank you for being the first person to show me that I do in fact matter and that all my wildest dreams are always within reach if I just try hard enough. Thank you for also teaching me that my life is more than just simply getting all A's in school.

To the Roper family, the single reason and motivation for my aspirations to have hope and happiness. Thank you for teaching me the real meaning of faith and that through God we are strong enough to overcome mountains.

To my namesake, Maudbel, otherwise known as B-Bell, though your body has left this earth, your love and wisdom remains in my heart, always.

And lastly, to, my best friend, Jesus for putting such amazing people in my life and for giving me the strength to push past my pain.

Introduction

I am not the first person to have said that every person has their own story, nor will I be the last.

That is pretty obvious. But I am going to say it anyway.

Every person has their own story. Every individual on this planet, all 7.28 billion of us, has had their own pasts, their own wounds, their own scars.

We have all faced Hell, and seen little pieces of heaven in our lives. In some way or another, we all are brought together as a community, in the midst of, simply put, life.

Every person on this earth, is bound together by that single truth. These everyday glimpses squeeze the breath out of our lungs, showing us the fierce realities that inhabit our lives. The hells that plague our world: war, poverty, starvation, abuse, and rape, to name a few, give us perspective and a purpose to fight against. And the slices of heaven: innocence, miracles, hope, faith, recovery, and triumph, prove that our efforts, to do right by the life we were given, were not in vain. Every person has their own story. Yes, some seemingly more challenging than others, but we all have a story.

These poems, are my story. I will not pretend to understand your life, nor will I try to convince you to sway your future decisions based off of my past experiences. These poems are just a part of my story. Flashes of heaven and hell.

For me, poetry has been the single most constant companion in my life. Each poem is a part of my heart, and my past, written plainly on a page for all to read; each poem is a heap of my raw emotions jumbled up into words that somehow make sense. These poems are a glimpse into my life and the lessons I have learned along the way. I have dealt with depression, loss, love, hope, hate, failure, faith, and chronic illness.

I am not the first person to experience what I have experienced.

I am not the first person to feel the emotions that have passed through my being.

And I am definitively not the first person to draw the same conclusions and perspectives that I have written down in my poems. That is pretty obvious. But I am going to say them anyway.

Everybody has their own story to tell. Here's mine.

POEM ONE

Will it Start With You?

People say there is evil in this world,
What are the evils of the world?
Really?
Genocide
Rape
Starvation
Homelessness
Tyranny
Conspiracy
Fear
Abuse
Corruption
Desertion

Think about that last word.
Desertion...
Desertion means to forsake and forget.

As a society, are we deserting the people that need us most
Are we deserting those who genocide is their life, not a topic of conversation
Are we deserting those who are a victim of rape
Are we deserting those who suffer from starvation
Are we deserting those who are left cold and homeless
Are we deserting those who fall into the hands of tyrants
Are we deserting those who are ruled by a government that is the foundation for conspiracy theories
Are we deserting those who are in perpetual fear
Are we deserting those who bear the gashes from abuse
Are we deserting those who have to look corruption in the eye
Are we deserting the deserted?

We have to stop staring at people as if they are less than people.

Rather, look at every victim in their eyes
See your guilt reflected back in your face.
Put yourself in their shoes.
Go outside,
In the bitter cold,
Dig yourself a hole in the ground,
And have your entire family live in that hole.
Only then, will you understand,
Even half of their everyday lives.
These children, men, women, and families are
Actual
People.
It is easier to turn the other cheek if you do not think of these people
As people, with actual
Hearts
And souls and minds and dreams.
We are the exact same down to the core,
Except for the location where we were unwillingly born.

We will never make any measureable, unwavering, difference,
If we continue to view their lives as less than our own.
So the question is,
What, or better said who, are the true evils in this world,

And will you let them win?

POEM TWO

Stand Tall Little One, You Do Make a Difference

Smokey shadows cast amongst walls
Their slinking figures barley identifiable

Light, laughter, and all things happiness
Are untraceable here.

Nightmares are living.
Dreams do not exist.

Burning anguish and gloom threaten innocent breaths
Aiming to suffocate all honestly pure minds.

Everything in the realm of darkness desires to consume the light
Illuminating the world.

The shining blaze comes from a single
White, waxy figure.

The flames, which burn bright,
Expose the varmints of the darkness.

The fire aglow cannot be diminished or touched, for
All the darkness in the world cannot even put out the light of a single little candle.

POEM THREE

You're Not Mine

My heart
Lunches
Forward.
Skips a
Beat.

                                        My heart
                                        Dissolves.

My body
Is numb.
Tingling
Down my neck
Down my toes.

                              I see you
                              Standing
                              There.
                              My knees
                              Buckle.
                              I swallow
                              Rocks.

I see you.
A smile escapes
My statue'd form
It dissolves.

                              I see you
                              Smile.
                              Then look
                              Down.
                              I hate
                              Myself.

You're not   You're not
Mine.   Mine.

You pass
Me.
You
Smile.

                    I pass you.
                    Your smile
                    Melts me.
                    I
                    Smile.

I smile back
Behind
My statue'd
Form.

                    You smile back. This
                    Is how it should be.

But, you're not   But, you're not
Mine.   Mine.

POEM FOUR

Possibilities

They are called The Innocents'.
There are millions of girls left, and abandoned.

All the others, the individuals who cannot comprehend, are called The Outsiders.

Three scenarios that express trillions of experiences.
Two possible outcomes that display the harrowing lives of millions of helpless girls.
One life, in this case, was forever altered.

But what about the rest?

Hollowed soul,
The Outsiders' call The Innocents'.

To be neglected,
At that young of an age,
The Outsiders' see as unimaginable.
Psychological impairment.
Forever tormented by
Past demons,
That will never cease,
Because those black creeping figures
No longer live only in nightmares.

The Outsiders' see whelping scars.
The Outsiders' see physical differences.
The Outsiders' see undesirableness.
The Outsiders' see The Innocent's pasts.

One scenario:
Abandoned, and unwanted.
Unloved; never caressed
By the soothing hand of
A mother.
Used, and empty.
Alone, even though the touch
Of a strange and cruel man
Awaits.
That is The Innocents' destiny.
To be sold.
That is The Innocents' worth,
In The Outsiders' eyes.
The Outsiders' see them.
The Innocents'.

And still do nothing.
The millions of
Faultless girls,
That are trapped,
Suffocated,
With no way out.

Lifeless girls
One dream,
Connects all The Innocents'
Together...

Blissful bubbly laughter that fills
Empty, past, voids.
Family
Belonging,
Finally wanted.
There remains no barriers,
No separation,
No contrariety,
Of outside appearance.
Love, that is so blinding-
That all whom are involved-
Can no longer see,
The physical differences.

The Outsiders' do not comprehend this complexity.
For they cannot live what
Was endured by The Innocents'.

They cannot experience
The depravity that could have taken place
If circumstances had turned out differently.

The Outsiders' ponder-
In their small-minded heads-
How could that be the case?
How could love have
No eyes,
No barriers,
No strings?
How could the undesireable, broken, Innocents' be
Boundlessly loved?

I answer,
How could they not?

POEM FIVE

Transitioning

I am a sand dollar.
My beauty is worshiped.
However, it is my story that should be recognized.

There I sit.
Up on my perch.
Overlooking the vast endless abyss
That The Humans call the Ocean.

I await for the day
Where the merciless blue
Demolishes my beautiful, fragile shell.

That is what I am.
A weak being.
An empty hollow frame.

One fateful evening,
A rip current seizes my unfilled skeleton.
Thrashing it about.
Powerless against the torment.

Suddenly the predatory grasp releases me.
Down.
Into the shivering, putrid black.
The vibrant blue vanishes.

I collapse on the jagged, sandy sea floor.
A situation only experienced in nightmares.
My brittle being,
Torn
Apart.

I am a crumpled sand dollar.
No more the beautiful creature
That The Humans worship.
I am broken.

But Then.
When it seemed all hope was lost.
A rouge wave again battered my body.

It thrust me back into the

Memorizing blue.
Without warning, something strange occurred.

Out of my mangled figure,
White dove-like bones flew on the current
Like a spirit floats on air.

It is then that I realize
That I never was simply just a
Hollow, beautiful, and frail shell.

I watch my past self
Being swiftly carried away.
My structure will be found
On a place The Humans call a beach.

When they find me,
Gazing at my deficiency,
Resting in their palms.
Their minds will ponder why
Such a magical and elusive creature
Could be made so fragile.

What they do not understand
Is we are much alike.
The Humans and I.

We were all made to break.
For it is inside udder brokenness

That we find strength in who we truly are.
The breathtaking outer shell is just that.
A shell.
Protecting the beauty inside.
The exterior form is only temporary;
However, the strength gained in letting go of one's past self
Will last a lifetime.

POEM SIX

The Lesson

"Life isn't fair"

Those powerful words
Echo in the minds of
Children
When situations do not go
Their way.

Children learn this harsh lesson
When their siblings
Eat the last cookie.

Or when they learn that
There will always be someone
Better than they are.

Over time, and with
Age,
Those same children who threw a fit
Over the minute details of the past,
Slowly learn that those words are capable of
Taking on a new meaning.

Those are words
Told to console teenagers
About the sinking feeling in their gut
From failure in school.

Or when they feel
Microscopic and
Unimportant because
Their crush does not hold
Their same endearing feelings
Towards them.

However, there comes a
Time when those words
Mean even more than
Thought possible.

People run around like
Ants on the ground.
Blindly following their
Leader, and completing
Their nonessential task
At hand.

However, there comes a
Time, when a bully stomps
On that ant hill,
And the world stops turning.
Only then, when the
Earth is completely still,
And utterly silent, that
The real truth behind
Those words are unmasked.

Those words take on
A new meaning when
Health starts
To fail.
The body
And mind that is supposed
To have adapted over billions
Of years to thrive.
The body that should be
The last line of defense.
Turns against them.
Cannot
Lean on anyone.

Or when the tragic truth
Comes to light,
That even sometimes
Hope,
Is not enough.

Or when
Clothes are painted all black,
And hearts and minds
Struggle to remember the
Face that turns stomachs
Into knots.
Their souls cry out into the
Open, crisp air.
Never again
Filling the empty void aching in their hearts.
Never again, knowing what it
feels like to not be
Alone.

What then?

It seems like then,
In that split second where
Everything alters forever,
that the once steady Earth
Spins like the tea cup
Ride at an amusement park.
It is in that moment,
That the words
"Life isn't fair" seem like a
Cruel joke.

What do you do when those
Words will never be as
Simple as they used to

Be?

When there seems
To be no consolation
For the pain felt.
What then?

Screw "life isn't fair."
Learn
What to do when life
Crashes down on top of
Them.
Suffocating.

A better phrase would read:
"Life isn't fair, so learn to fight like hell."

POEM SEVEN

Perspective on Perception

The Sun, illuminates the world below
Against the pillows which we call clouds
And amongst the blanket of blue which we call the sky.

The Sun, hangs rich above our heads
Silently casting down its bidding
To the world below.

The heavenly light in all its high glory,
Controls our very lives and everything in which mankind
Takes for granted.

Without it's light humans could not live, and Earth,
The place we call home,
Would be cast into the consuming, clouded, black, endless oblivion.

Compared to the vastness of the Sun,
The Moon stands small,
However, its comparable size does not mean The Moon is powerless.

In and of itself, The Moon controls
The forceful and mighty swells of the oceans tides,
Which, in fact, cover the majority of Earth.

The Moon sends its commands
And guides populations of species, all around the world, to meet in one place at one perfect time.
These capabilities are just some of the things that The Moon holds power over.

The Moon does not idly rest upon
The blackness of night, nor does it simply dance
With the twinkling stars that loom above.

The Moon carries the same heavy pressure—
the burden of being the guiding light for simple minded beings—
As the Sun does.

Thus it can be concluded,
That physical size does not determine the amount
Of impact of change on lives.
Now, I ask that you use this same level of thinking...

Compared to the sheer size of The Moon,
One single, miniscule human being
Is incomparable.

However, because size does not matter,
I ask,
What amount of immeasurable change is one human capable of?

POEM EIGHT

An Everlasting Remembrance

I remember the days I lived as a flower.
When I wilted and withered away when the sun was missing,
And then felt bright and alive when the sun was found.

I remember when I felt the sun's glow kiss my petals,
Filling me up with its warmness and joy.

I remember dancing and playing with the wind,
Feeling its touch blow my sorrows away.

I remember feeling the rain's fury when it pelted me with its watery bullets.

I remember the feeling of the ground under my roots,
The soft warm feeling giving me life and firmness,
Giving me a place that I will always call home.

I remember the day that my winged friend visited me for the first time,
When we talked forever with care and ease.

I remember the day I could no longer feel anything.
The sun's touch
dancing with the wind
The rain's watery fury
The cold solid ground
My winged friend talking to me.
The last thought I had before I was taken to a better place was,
I will always remember the days I was a flower.

POEM NINE

The One

Trash.
Piled up into enormous heaps.

Lost things
Thrown away
Forever forgotten.

Putrid smell
From all of the decaying inhabitants
Living and dead.

Mountain
Of things that pollute our world.
The sun
Never shines its' glow here.

The rain

Never washes away the ghastly.
Clouds
Always consume
Darkness.

On top of that pile,
A bluebonnet grows.

It's blue petals
Contrasting colors against
Darkness.

Something so
Atrocious
Should never experience
Exquisiteness.

Nevertheless it grew
And made the
Trash
Less like trash
Piled up into enormous heaps.

No more lost things
Thrown away
Forgotten forever.

No more
Putrid smell or
Mountains of trash.

It was still a
Trash pile,
However now, there was
A sliver of heaven atop.

The sun shone,
The rain washed away the ghastly,
There were no more clouds to consume it with
Darkness.

There the bluebonnet still stays,
Growing taller every day.

With its steady growth,
Comes a sensation of awe.
A miracle
That was created out of faith, love and hope.

POEM TEN

The Perfect Love Story

I wonder who the lighting calls out to
When the sky is dark
And the clouds roll always.

Does she call out
To nobody in particular
In Morse code

Does she hope
That someone out there
May just see her light

Does she try to hold onto
Something perfect
To only have it turn into a storm

Does she give it all she has
Then when nobody comes
Fades away into the darkness

Does she feel hopeless
For her one and only true love
She can never touch

                I wonder who the thunder calls out to
                        When the sky is dark
                      And the clouds roll away

                      Does he constantly search
                            The night sky
                  In hopes he would find her

        Does he scream in the middle of the night
                          Trying, reaching
          For something he knows he cannot have

                      Does he hope that someone
                          Might just look up
                      And actually hear him

Does he cry into the
Dark and silent night
Feeling desperate and empty

Does he feel hopeless
For his one and only true love
He can never touch

Do they feel hopeless
For their one and only true love
They can never touch.

When you look into the abyss
That is the dark night sky
And hear and see their pleas

Do you feel their sorrow
When the rain
Cries for their two love stories

Do you wish that you
Could have their love story...
Not the type in fairytales
But the true kind,
The kind that cannot be
Severed by distance
The kind that can
Survive the storm
The kind that never looses
Their passion due to time

The kind that never loses hope
Even though their one and only true love
They can never touch.

POEM ELEVEN

Wondering About Wondering

Why do people dream
If they say that dreams don't come true?

Why does the moon shine so bright every night
Only to be outshone by the sun the next day?

I always wondered why people hope
If they don't give hope to others?

Why do flowers try to stretch and reach the sun

When they know they will never reach it?

Why do we feel bad for the world
When we have the power to fix it?

Why do the waves crash upon the sand
Only to be pulled back to sea?

Why do little kids build sand castles on the beach
When they know that what they built will be destroyed?

Why does fire want to consume everything?
Does it make it feel better; leaving a wake of destruction in its path?

Why do people want to be birds so they can fly away?
Escaping.
When really either way, when it's the right season, they will be coming back to where they started anyway?

I always wondered why people wonder,
When we could be out doing more with our mind
Then sitting and wondering?

POEM TWELVE

What You Left Behind

When I think of you
I think of bright yellow sunflowers
Floating against the vast sky.
When I think of you
I think of sitting on your lap, in that
plushy blue chair
Reading Winnie the Pooh.
When I think of you
I think of us always laughing at each other
and you'd end up saying
That I was from a zoo.

I remember being loved
So much by you, that you'd gallop like horse
Around the hallways, I didn't even have to shove.
I remember being loved
So much by you that you would call me a nut
I would say you were the tree I fell from, neither of us budged.
I remember being loved
So much by you that during Christmas time
You gave me a turtledove.

As fierce as the sun
With everything you did, you reminded me that our
Love could never be undone.
As fierce as the sun
With everything you did, you taught me
To love everyone.
As fierce as the sun
With everything you did, you showed me that with love,
The game of life will be won.

As strong as a knight
You engraved in my mind, that happiness is the only key to life that will ensure that you will fly like a kite.
As strong as a knight

You engraved in my mind, that God can and will always be
The light.
As strong as a knight
You engraved in my mind, that the only thing that really matters
Is your might.

As sweet as honey
You always reminded me, that there is more to
Life than money.
As sweet as honey
You always reminded me, to illuminate
The world, and make it forever sunny.
As sweet as honey
You always reminded me, that a best friend is always
Someone who can be my type of funny.

You were my rock
That always stayed, just like the
Old singing clock.
You were my rock
That always stayed, and showed me that when a door
Shuts in your face, just knock.
You were my rock
That always stayed, to teach me that when faced with a problem

The best thing you can do is talk.

You were my saving grace
That never failed, to guide me
And show me to always leave a trace.
You were my saving grace
That never failed, to teach me
That life is like a vase.
You were my saving grace
That never failed, to put me
In my rightful place.

When I think of you, I remember being loved as fierce as the sun, strong as a night, as sweet as honey; you were my rock, you were my saving grace; and with every breath, you took my heart forever, and you showed me what everlasting love really is.

POEM THIRTEEN

Live Through It

To cause pain, or simply live in it?
Pain is a misunderstood word that is used to convey
a wide variety of instances that should not be connected at all.
However, it is the only word used to describe the
Beautiful travesty that connects every person in this world together.
Pain is the train wreck of life that causes deep, gut wrenching
Tears to tear their way out of eyes
because the fire burning inside cannot be put out.
Pain is the bloated, starving tummies of children that cannot remember
What food feels or looks like in their

mouths.
Pain is the never ceasing, blood curdling, ear piercing sounds of war,
that have an eerily, silent aura looming about.
Pain is seeing the perfect, sunny, and smiling world outside,
but knowing that you can never join it.
As humans, it is not the physical act of pain that hurts us,
it is the questioning, and thinking that follows.
Pain is an act, an emotion that all humans experience.
But why? Why us?
Why is there death? Why is their rape? Why is there starvation?
Why is their disease? Why is there genocide?
Why is there desertion? Why is there pain at all?
That is the most painful and hard question that all humans ask: Why?
Also, perhaps, the most uncertain question that people of faith ask is:
Why would a loving God, cause love to cease?
But does, He, or perhaps the universe, actually cause love to cease?
He goes down from Heaven and manipu-

lates the world to make bad things to happen?
Does He?
Or do bad things just happen, and as humans, we personalize situations,
and blow it all out of proportion?
Maybe, just maybe, instead of blaming the universe, or God, we should place
the blame on ourselves?
As humans we ask too many questions.
Pain is just that, pain.
Why must humans personalize, and question and overthink-
when we were really made not to seek out the truth,
but simply live in it?
We were made to experience pain,
Not to question it.
Pain is a phase, a lapse in time, an event never ceasing,
and we were made to live through it.

MIABEL J. SELF

About The Author

Miabel has been fighting like hell since she was in the third grade when she was diagnosed with auditory dyslexia, all the way to now, continuing to have strength through another, different, life-altering disease. Poetry had become Miabel's outlet in the sixth grade, which forever altered her perspective on life—and gave her hope at last. Her poetry perspective brings young women hope nationwide. She lives in San Antonio, TX with her family and two dogs named Ding Dong and Bailey. Find Miabel at poetsperspective.com.

Made in the USA
Coppell, TX
23 May 2022